THRILL SEEKERS

RUNNING WITH THE BULLS

BY CLAIRE FLYNN

Gareth Stevens
Publishing

Please visit our website, www.garethstevens.com. For a free color catalog of all our high-quality books, call toll free 1-800-542-2595 or fax 1-877-542-2596.

Library of Congress Cataloging-in-Publication Data

Flynn, Claire E.
Running with the bulls / by Claire E. Flynn.
   p. cm. — (Thrill seekers)
Includes index.
ISBN 978-1-4824-3294-7 (pbk.)
ISBN 978-1-4824-3295-4 (6-pack)
ISBN 978-1-4824-0169-1 (library binding)
1. Running the bulls — Spain — Pamplona. 2. Pamplona (Spain). 3. Bull racing. I. Flynn, Claire E. II. Title.
GV1108.4 F59 2014
791.82—dc23

First Edition

Published in 2014 by
Gareth Stevens Publishing
111 East 14th Street, Suite 349
New York, NY 10003

Copyright © 2014 Gareth Stevens Publishing

Designer: Michael J. Flynn
Editor: Therese Shea

Photo credits: Cover, pp. 1, 9, 10 AFP/Getty Images; p. 4 Olinchuk/Shutterstock.com; pp. 5, 11, 17, 21 Pedro Armestre/AFP/Getty Images; p. 7 Digital Globe/Getty Images; p. 13 Migel/Shutterstock.com; pp. 15, 19, 22 Pablo Blazquez Dominguez/Getty Images; pp. 16, 25, 26, 27 Rafa Rivas/AFP/Getty Images; p. 23 Jasper Juinen/Getty Images; p. 29 Joshua Lott/Getty Images.

Printed in the United States of America

CPSIA compliance information: Batch #CW14GS: For further information contact Gareth Stevens, New York, New York at 1-800-542-2595.

CONTENTS

Words in the glossary appear in **bold** type
the first time they are used in the text.

READY, SET, RUN

Running with a dozen fierce bulls down a crowded street may sound like your worst nightmare. For some, it's not only an adventure, it's a yearly **tradition**. They truly enjoy it, too! During the event called the Running of the Bulls, hundreds of people try to stay a step ahead of bulls set loose in the streets. Does that sound fun or frightening? It's a little of both according to the **participants**!

Each year, the Running of the Bulls takes place during the **Fiesta de San Fermín**—or Festival of Saint Fermín—in Pamplona, Spain. The fiesta begins at noon on July 6 and ends at midnight on July 14.

Time to Celebrate

The Fiesta de San Fermín isn't just about a bull run. It was originally meant to honor Pamplona's first **bishop**. Now, people from all over the world take part in a celebration that includes dancing, singing, and fireworks. They even have a parade in which they carry giant heads that represent kings and queens.

The Running of the Bulls starts on July 7 and is held each day until the festival ends.

HOW IT ALL BEGAN

In 1592, the Fiesta de San Fermín was moved from September to July, but the Running of the Bulls may date back as far as the 1200s. The event was a way to move bulls from a Pamplona **corral** into the bullfighting ring. The bulls ran, and people on the streets shouted and used sticks to send them in the right direction.

People didn't begin actually running with the bulls until the 1800s. Historians think that the butchers of Pamplona were once responsible for bringing the bulls into the ring. For some reason, townspeople began to join them, running in front. It became more and more popular each year.

The Encierro

What was once a local festival is now one that people from all over the world come to see or take part in. The Spanish call the Running of the Bulls the *Encierro*. There's a run each full day of the festival, totaling seven runs in all.

This map shows the streets (*calles*) and other sites along the Running of the Bulls route.

bullring

Telefónica stretch

Calle Estafeta

Calle Mercaderes

town hall square

hill of Santo Domingo

bull corral

ON YOUR MARK

Every morning during the Fiesta de San Fermín, thrill seekers gather in the street. Many runners wear all white clothes with red scarves tied around their neck and waist. They also carry rolled-up newspapers to wave or hit the bulls.

Participants sing and chant to Saint Fermín, asking to be guided safely on their run. They use Spanish as well as the Basque language that's spoken in northeastern Spain. When the songs are finished, they say, "*Viva San Fermín,*" which means "long live Saint Fermín" in Spanish. After the runners see the signal, they begin running for their lives!

Seeing Red

Did you know bulls are color-blind? The reason runners wear red around their waists and necks isn't to make the bulls angry, like many people think. The red is said to honor Saint Fermín. They may wear white for him, too. Others say runners are dressed to look like the butchers who began the run years ago.

The runners also say, "*Gora San Fermín,*" which means "long live Saint Fermín" in the Basque language.

AND THEY'RE OFF!

Several rockets are fired during the Running of the Bulls to signal important events. The first rocket goes off at 8 a.m. to tell the runners the corral gate is about to open. The second rocket tells runners that all the bulls are on the streets. The third rocket means that all the bulls have made it into the bullring, and the final rocket is fired when the bulls are in the pens. The *Encierro* is then finished, and the rest of the day's events begin.

The bull run usually only lasts 3 or 4 minutes. However, there's a lot of excitement packed into that short time.

rocket

This photo shows that crowds increase the danger for the runners. People may not be able to move out of the way when they need to.

Tips for the Run

It's said that bulls look to the right at the beginning of the run, so it's best for the runner to stay as far to the left as possible to increase their chances of a safe run. Also, a runner is no safer behind a bull than in front. Bulls can—and sometimes do—turn around.

FENCED IN

The entire bull run is about 1/2 mile (825 m). You may be wondering how the bulls are kept on track on the way to the bullfighting ring. A long wooden fence is assembled along the run using more than 3,000 pieces of wood.

Part of the fence is left up throughout the entire festival, while other sections are put together and taken apart each day of the event. The buildings of Pamplona also act as barriers. Besides keeping the bulls contained, the fence and buildings keep the thousands of onlookers cheering for the runners safe.

Safety First

Spanish Red Cross (or *Cruz Roja*) stations are set up at certain points along the route. When a runner is injured or needs to be rescued for any reason, they're pulled through spaces in the wooden fence. The fence keeps the Red Cross workers safe from the bulls, too!

You can see from the photo that the space between the fence rails is big enough for a person to squeeze through, but not a bull!

CONTAINING THE BEASTS

The *pastores* play one of the most important roles in the Running of the Bulls. *Pastor* means "shepherd" in Spanish, and *pastores* act like shepherds. They herd the bulls and help keep onlookers safe.

Between eight and 10 *pastores* run with the bulls. They all dress alike and carry sticks. They run behind the herd to make sure the animals stay together and that one bull doesn't stray from the others. This also prevents a bull from turning around and heading back towards the corral or just stopping. *Pastores* also keep the runners away from any bull that may have separated from the group.

These Guys Are Good

Each *pastor* is responsible for about 300 feet (91 m) of the run. They wear green to make themselves stand out from the crowd. *Pastores* are bull experts, but many of them have other professions that don't have anything to do with bulls, like fishing and farming.

You can see the *pastor* at the bottom of this photo, guiding the bulls down the street.

PASTORES

The bulls have a lot of energy, even at the end of the run. Until the bulls are placed in the pens, there's still danger to the runners in the bullfighting ring. This is where the *dobladores* play their important role. They guide bulls and runners once they enter the ring at the end of the run. They direct the runners to the sides of the ring and the bulls into pens.

There are usually four *dobladores* in the bullring. They're usually former bullfighters, so they know quite a bit about bulls. Each one carries a cape to attract the bulls.

Dobladores work so that bulls don't attack runners, as is seen in this photo.

The *dobladores* wait in the center of the ring for the bulls, while the runners quickly move to the sides.

Watch the Cape

Dobladores are careful about how they use their capes to get the bulls into their pens. The bulls are used in bullfights, so the *dobladores* drag the cape on the ground. If the cape was lifted, the bulls might try to charge, tiring them out, and making the later bullfighting contest unfair.

NOT ALL BULL

Although the event is called the Running of the Bulls, only six animals are actually bulls. The other six are steers. Bulls are cattle used for **breeding**. Steers are cattle raised for meat. There are differences in their behavior, too. Bulls can be quite **vicious**. Steers are usually calm. In fact, the presence of the steers calms the bulls, which keeps the runners just a bit safer on the way to the ring.

Whether it's a steer or a bull following you, the sound of heavy hooves and the sight of sharp horns behind you can be pretty scary!

Steer Clear

The six bulls are released from the corral first. The whole herd runs at a speed of 15 miles (24 km) per hour. When some runners find out they were running with a steer instead of a bull, they feel **embarrassed**. Bulls are much fiercer beasts than steers. Which would you rather run with?

One of the biggest dangers to runners is the sharp horns of the bulls! Steers usually don't try to attack people.

NOT A FUN RUN

Being chased by fierce bulls isn't everyone's idea of fun! This event is only for someone who's willing to risk injury or even death. Since 1924, when they began keeping records, more than a dozen people have been killed in Pamplona during the Running of the Bulls.

One of these was a 22-year-old American named Matthew Tassio. He was knocked to the ground by a bull. Tassio didn't follow one of the rules of the run: "If you go down, you stay down." Instead of lying on the ground, he got up again. Another bull charged at him, and he was stabbed with its horn.

Stay Low

Runners are expected to learn the tips and tricks of a successful bull run. You might be surprised that you're not supposed to get up during the bull run if you fall. However, it's better to be tripped over or even kicked by a bull than **gored**.

By staying down, these fallen runners have a better chance of not getting severely injured by a bull's horns.

Each year, hundreds of people are injured during the Running of the Bulls. Luckily, most injuries aren't serious and result from falling, not a run-in with a bull. The roads of the route are made out of cobblestone and can be slippery. And people have to worry about their fellow runners just as much as the big beasts. In their hurry to get out of the way, other runners can **trample** those who have fallen.

Runners should be physically fit and should take every **precaution** for their own safety. It's a good idea to train for this event as runners do for other types of runs.

It's important to be aware of what's going on all around you when you're a participant in the Running of the Bulls.

Imagine hearing the thunder of the bulls' hooves or feeling their hot breath on your back!

Who Can Run?

Although most of the runners are men, women can and do run with the bulls. Almost anyone can participate in this event as long as they're at least 18 years old. Once, a father ran with his 10-year-old son! The family was lucky to escape with a fine and their lives.

IN THE RING

Maybe you can imagine running away from a bull, but what about staying in the ring with one? The bullfight after each day's run is broken into three parts. The first is when the bullfighter, called a matador, uses a cape to show off the bull's qualities. Is it fast, angry, and ready to fight? The matador watches how the bull behaves and learns how it charges and turns.

In the second part of the fight, the matador's assistants place darts in the bull's back. These are supposed to make the bull, who may be tiring, even angrier. The third part is the fight to the death. The matador kills the bull with a sword.

Tickets for Sale

There are almost 20,000 seats available to view the bullfight, but most of the tickets for the fight belong to season ticket holders. Fewer than 2,000 tickets are available to be purchased by the public. However, some season ticket holders sell their tickets on the streets.

The events continue in the bullfighting ring after the
Running of the Bulls.

IS IT WRONG?

Unsurprisingly, animal rights **activists** are against many of the events of the Fiesta de San Fermín. PETA (People for the Ethical Treatment of Animals) says that the bulls are mistreated. They're scared by the crowds, the unfamiliar city streets, and being hit by newspapers and *pastores'* sticks. PETA is angered by the killing of the bulls in the bullfights as well.

Many people say that the events are tradition and should continue as they have for centuries. But PETA says many traditions have changed and this one should, too. What do you think? Should the Running of the Bulls and the bullfights carry on?

Truth: Bullfighting is Cruel

Matadors don't just kill bulls, they perform certain moves and are judged according to their daring and grace.

A Fair Fight?

In the final part of the bullfight, the matador uses a red and yellow cape attached to a wooden sword to tire out the bull. Once the bull seems tired, the bullfighter switches to a steel sword. He spears the bull in the back. The crowd and the president of the bullfighting ring decide if it was a "good fight."

SIMILAR THRILLS

People don't have to go all the way to Spain if they want to run with the bulls. They can find a bull run right here in the United States. There are "mock bull runs," where a few people dress up like bulls and chase participants who are dressed like the runners at the Fiesta de San Fermín!

The Great Bull Run uses real bulls and is held in various cities around the nation. It's not quite Pamplona, but it's still pretty thrilling—and dangerous. People have been sent to the hospital in the past. Would you want to participate in this run or even the *Encierro*? Just don't forget the many dangers that accompany these thrills!

Pig and Sheep Runs?

Bulls aren't the only animals people like to run with. In Ireland, there's a pig run, where people run with wild boars. In New Zealand, there's a "running of the sheep" in which people run with more than a thousand sheep down the main street in a small farm town.

People in other countries try to capture the sense of excitement of Pamplona's bull run, but there's only one *Encierro*!

GLOSSARY

activist: one who acts strongly in support of or against an issue

bishop: one who leads the members of a church in a certain area

breeding: mating and giving birth

corral: a pen for livestock

embarrass: to become or cause somebody to be ashamed or ill at ease

fiesta: the Spanish word for party

gore: to harm a person or animal with horns or tusks

participant: someone who takes part in something

precaution: an action taken in advance to protect against harm or trouble

tradition: a long-practiced custom

trample: to injure by stepping heavily on something or someone

vicious: dangerous and intending to do harm by fighting

FOR MORE INFORMATION

BOOKS

Crosbie, Duncan. *Find Out About Spain*. Hauppauge, NY: Barrons Educational Series, 2006.

Croy, Anita. *Spain*. Washington, DC: National Geographic, 2010.

WEBSITES

Running of the Bulls
www.kidzworld.com/article/7913-running-of-the-bulls
Read more about this dangerous event.

Running of the Bulls
www.bullrunpamplona.com/
Find out much more about the San Fermín festival and the Running of the Bulls.

What Is a Bull-Fight?
www.sanfermin.com/index.php/en/la-fiesta/corrida/
Learn about the bullfights and other events in Pamplona.

INDEX